MEET THE
ORCHESTRA

MEET THE ORCHESTRA

WILLIAM W. SUGGS
pictures by Enrico Arno

THE MACMILLAN COMPANY, NEW YORK
COLLIER-MACMILLAN LIMITED, LONDON

The Macmillan Company, New York
Collier-Macmillan Canada, Ltd., Toronto, Ontario
Library of Congress catalog card number: 66-11110
Printed in the United States of America
First Printing

CONTENTS

INTRODUCTION:
AT THE ORCHESTRA CONCERT

The hall is a confusion of sound. High notes and low notes, squeaks and squawks, bangs and booms—everyone plays at once. We hear the shrill, piercing notes of the piccolo against the deep rumble of the double bass, and here and there a recognizable snatch of melody. An ear-splitting blast from the trumpet cuts through the blur. What is going on? The orchestra is tuning up!

We have come to hear our favorite symphony, and we know that in a few moments all will be calm and orderly. We can soon settle back in our seats to listen, and to enjoy what we hear. For whether it is classical, "pops," or jazz, it is all part of our great music, the music of the orchestra.

But what is the story behind a concert like this? How can we explain this remarkable assembly of musicians, all playing together so pleasantly? Making sense with sound —making music—is the job of musical instruments and the people who play them. In the orchestra, a great number and variety of musical instruments—and their players —come together to make what we can think of as one gigantic instrument. Before the conductor enters and brings about this transformation, let's take a look at the individuals on whom he will work his magic.

HOW MUSIC IS MADE

When you listen to music, you are listening to a special kind of sound, different from the various sounds and noises you ordinarily hear around you. All sounds begin when something vibrates—that is, when it moves very quickly back and forth. But to make a musical sound the vibration has to be even, the same number of back-and-forth movements occurring each second.

The speed of this vibration also makes a difference in the sound produced. When something vibrates only a few times each second, it makes a very low, deep sound. When it vibrates very quickly, the sound is high and shrill. The lowness or highness of a sound is called its pitch.

But even when instruments play a note of the same pitch, each one seems to have its own musical sound or voice. There are two reasons for this. First, instruments are built differently; some are made of metal, some of wood, some are long and narrow, some short and wide, and each of these things causes the instrument to vibrate in its own distinctive way.

The second reason is that different instruments actually produce their vibrations differently. In the orchestra there are three families of instruments, and each produces musical sound by its own method. The first family, the string section, produces sound by the plucking or scraping of strings to make them vibrate. With the second group, the wind instruments—woodwinds and brass—it is the air inside each instrument which is made to vibrate. The third group, the percussion instruments, is made up of instruments which vibrate when the player hits them.

When all the instruments of the orchestra are playing at the same time, the sight is a strange one indeed. We see the string players scraping with their bows, the wind players blowing into curious tubes, and the percussion players in the back row, banging away. It is hard to believe that all these different and sometimes odd-looking motions can produce such beautiful music.

You don't need a musical instrument to make musical sound. These three simple "instruments"—percussion, wind, and string—will produce perfectly good musical tone. The shattered glass is vibrating unevenly; it produces just plain noise.

Different pitches are produced in the bottles by the different lengths of vibrating air. The pitch of the plucked rubber bands is affected by their thickness, length, and tautness. Only one tone is possible with the tapped glass at left.

THE STRING SECTION

The string section is the backbone of the orchestra—the largest, most important single group of instruments. In a modern orchestra almost two thirds of the musicians are string players. Because of the importance of the section, its members sit right at the front of the stage, where they can see the conductor clearly and where their sound won't be drowned out by the blare of the brass.

There are five different kinds of string instruments. Four of them—the violin, the viola, the violoncello, and the double bass—are members of the violin family. The fifth is the harp.

The violin family of today developed from the viols, a group of instruments used during the Middle Ages by the troubadours who traveled from town to town singing and playing to earn a living. The viols were rather strange instruments, a little like guitars in appearance but played with a bow. They were made in nine or ten different sizes, the largest being the great bass viol, which was so large that two men were needed to play it—one man to bow while the other pushed down the strings to change the pitch.

Unlike the four-stringed instruments of the modern violin family, these early viols usually had six strings. But they were made to produce different musical tones in basically the same way. Each string on a viol (as on a violin, viola, cello, or bass) was tuned to a different note, or pitch. The player could get other notes from the same string by holding it down with his fingers. This shortened the string, made it vibrate faster, and produced a higher pitch.

As time went by musicians found that they could play all the existing viol music without using every type of viol. In fact, they found it much more convenient to use only four sizes—a small viol, a medium-sized one, a large, and a very large viol. Instrument makers began to concentrate on these and let the others fall into neglect. With the discovery that they could get a purer sound by making their instruments wider and more rounded in shape, the modern violin family was born.

Between 1650 and 1750 a group of violin makers in the little Italian town of Cremona produced some of the finest stringed instruments ever made. Even today, most of our violins, violas, cellos, and double basses are copies of these early Italian instruments. The most famous member of this group was Antonius Stradivarius. Stradivarius worked painstakingly to assure that each violin he made was as perfect as possible, and he often spent more than a month completing just one instrument. Several hundred "Strads" are still in use today, and many of our finest artists perform on instruments crafted by the great master of Cremona.

A great variety of stringed instruments contributed to the development of our modern violin family. This group from about 1560 includes, from left to right, a tenor viol, a contraviolone, a violino, and a violone, forerunners of the viola, the double bass, the violin, and the cello. The little ridges, or frets, running across the fingerboards of these instruments helped the player place his fingers correctly when making changes of pitch. Frets are still found on guitars and banjos.

THE VIOLIN

The violin is the smallest of the stringed instruments; in fact it takes its name from the Italian word meaning "small viol." The violin is almost as beautiful to look at as it is to listen to. It is carved by hand from very fine rare woods, and more than seventy separate pieces go into each instrument.

The violin's four strings, which are usually made of steel wire, or silver wire wrapped around nylon, are stretched tightly over the bridge and wound on four pegs on its neck. To tune his instrument, the violinist adjusts the tension on the strings by means of these pegs; a taut string gives a higher pitch than a looser one. When the violin is played continuously, or when it remains idle for any length of time, the strings tend to loosen so that the tone goes flat. The last thing a violinist—or any string player—does before a performance is tune up, and he will probably have

Out of a bewildering variety of stringed instruments, the violin (with its family) emerged to replace them all. A violin bow and mute are shown opposite. The viola and cello use basically the same bow, with small differences in weight and length.

to stop several times during the concert to bring a slack string up to pitch.

Early violins were played with curved implements that looked much like hunting bows. These first bows were very crude, and hard to use. It was almost a hundred years after Stradivarius built his fine violins that a French violin maker, François Tourte, invented the type of bow in use today. He made his bow from Pernambuco wood, a light springy wood found only in Brazil; to string it, he used bleached horsehair, clamping some 150 strands on each bow.

When the violinist draws his bow across the strings of his violin, the rough hair makes the strings vibrate, and produces sound. To keep the bow hair rough, the violinist rubs it with a little cake of rosin that he keeps in his violin case. There is also a little screw at the end of the bow which may be turned to adjust the tension on the bow hairs. If the hairs are too loose, the bow makes a very scratchy sound on the strings.

The violin is a valuable instrument in the orchestra because it can do such a variety of things well. Its usual tone is brilliant and singing, but the player can make it sound vigorous, tender, and even ghostly. To make the violin sound especially soft, the violinist uses a little clamp called a mute, which fits tightly onto the bridge to lessen the vibrations of the strings.

Violinists can play without the bow by just plucking the strings. They can even play two notes at once, by drawing the bow across two strings simultaneously. The violin has a very wide range; in other words, it can play very high notes and low notes as well.

Because it is such a versatile instrument, and because its

tone blends so well with the others, there are more violins in the orchestra than any other single instrument. In most orchestras there are twenty-five or thirty violinists, divided into two groups. The first violinists usually play the main melody, while the second violinists play a less featured part, filling out the harmony or supplying an accompanying melody.

The leader of the first violin section is called the concertmaster. Next to the conductor he is the most important member of the orchestra. He is often called upon to play solos, and even to substitute for the conductor. One famous orchestra, when their conductor became ill, played several concerts alone, with no one directing from the podium, just by following the exaggerated bow movements of the concertmaster.

THE VIOLA

From a distance, the violin and the viola look so much alike that they are hard to tell apart. Actually the viola—the next largest member of the violin family—is about one-seventh larger than the violin. Its shape and construction are basically the same, and it is made of the same type of wood. The player holds the instrument under his chin, as he would a violin.

The four strings of the viola are tuned five notes lower than the strings of a violin. The tone of the instrument is soft, mellow and somewhat sad, and has a blending effect in the string section. The viola is usually called upon to play harmonizing parts and to help fill out the orchestral sound. There are normally eight to ten violists in an orchestra.

THE VIOLONCELLO

The word violoncello comes from the Italian *violone*, the word for the double bass (the largest stringed instrument), and *cello*, a word ending meaning small. The violoncello, or cello as it is now called, is just that—a small double bass. It is twice the size of the viola—much too large to be held under the chin like its smaller brothers, or on the knee like the ancient viols. Instead, the cellist holds the instrument between his knees, with its body propped up off the floor by a little metal rod called an end pin. The neck end points upward and toward him, just the reverse of the violin and viola playing positions.

The modern cello is shaped like the violin and viola, but is proportionally deeper back to front. It developed from a strange-looking instrument called the *viola da gamba*, which is Italian for leg or knee viol. The viola da gamba was larger than the viola but smaller than the cello, and was held upright on the player's knee. But the viola da gamba just didn't work. It was much too big and clumsy to be played in such a position, and too small to produce low notes of much power. As time went by, viol builders began making larger and larger instruments, and the modern cello was invented. It was not until the early 1700's, however, that it found a place in the orchestra.

The strings of the cello are tuned eight notes lower than those of the viola, and the tone of the instrument is deep and powerful. Yet its range is much wider than the viola's, and it is capable of producing very high notes as well. The cello is an important member of the orchestra because it adds a rich, deep sound to the string section. Most orchestras use from ten to twelve cellos.

THE DOUBLE BASS

The largest stringed instrument is the double bass. It stands about six feet tall. To play this giant, the player must stand up or sit on a special high stool. Like the cello, the body of the bass rests on the floor on an end pin and the neck points upward.

The bass is the only stringed instrument which is still shaped like the old viols. It has sloping sides, a flat back, and a high bridge. The bow of the bass is wide and curved like the old viol bow.

The four strings of the double bass are made of steel or silver wire, wound around nylon. They are very thick and hard, and the bass player must have strong fingers to push them down.

There are usually eight to ten bass players in the orchestra. The deep, rumbling voice of the instrument helps balance the sound of the higher strings and adds power to the sound of the whole section.

Apart from its role as an orchestral instrument, the double bass has another life as a regular member of jazz groups. Here it may play an occasional solo, but usually it is plucked, instead of bowed, to provide a low, pulsing background to the free melodic wanderings of the other instruments.

THE HARP

The harp is the oldest instrument in the string section. When Stone Age man found that his bow string made a sound as the arrow left it, he added several strings to his weapon to make different sounds. Next, he attached to the bow frame a little sound box (something like an echo chamber) that vibrated along with the strings and made the tone louder. The ordinary hunting bow had become a true harp.

The ancient Egyptians used beautiful harps inlaid with gold and ivory to accompany singing and dancing. As time went by more and more strings were added to harps until there were so many that the instrument became difficult to play. Finally, in 1810, a French piano maker named Sébastien Érard built a new harp. This harp had pedals that changed the tuning of the strings automatically, making it easy to play in any key. Érard's invention is still in use today.

The modern harp has forty-seven steel and nylon strings and seven pedals, and stands about five feet high. The harpist plucks the strings with the fingers of both hands (all but the fifth finger, which is never used). To help him find his way around this forest of strings, different colors are used; some strings are red, some are purple, and others white. The harp frame is made of strong wood and is often decorated with gold.

The harp is a special member of the string section. Though certainly a string instrument, it is outside the violin family to which all the others belong. The sound from its plucked strings—soft and silvery—is quite different in character from the sound of the bowed string instruments.

The harp is not always used with the orchestra; in fact, very few composers have written for this instrument at all. Even when the harp is included in the orchestra, only one is usually called for, and it will most likely be used sparingly in the course of a composition.

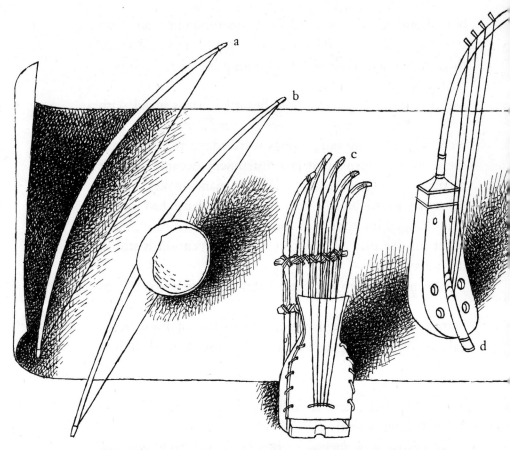

The evolution of the harp begins with the simple hunting bow (a), still used in Africa as a musical instrument. The bow is held near the player's mouth, which serves to magnify the sound. The next step (b) was to attach a gourd to act as a sound chamber. Stage three (c) combined several bows with one sound box to obtain different pitches. The strings of this clumsy instrument had to be tuned by winding them around the individual bow ends. Next (d), many strings were attached to one bow, with tuning pegs for easier winding. One problem remained: as one string was tuned the bow flexed, throwing the others out of tune. A brace was added to strengthen the frame, and the modern harp was achieved. The Irish harp (e) is of modern type, though smaller than today's instrument (f).

e

f

STRING GROUPS AND CHAMBER MUSIC

In all orchestras, the string section sits near the front of the stage, where the players can see the conductor most clearly. In many orchestras the seats are arranged so that the first and second violin sections are side by side, with the violas, cellos, and double basses opposite. Sometimes, the first and second violinists sit facing each other on different sides of the stage, with the violas, cellos, and basses in the center. Many conductors feel that this arrangement makes the sound of the string section more balanced.

The stringed instruments are used not only as a part of the full orchestra with the wind and percussion sections; sometimes the string section of the orchestra plays by itself. Then it is known as a string orchestra. There are usually thirty to forty-five players in such a group. Many composers have written music for the string orchestra because they liked its soft, sweet sound.

Even before the big symphony orchestra came to be, kings and noblemen would frequently hire small groups of musicians to play private concerts and at parties and dinners. Music for these groups was called chamber music, because it was always played in a small room or chamber.

Chamber-music groups may be made up of brass, woodwind, and percussion instruments, and even combinations among them, but all-string groups are perhaps most favored by composers and music lovers alike. One of the most popular chamber groups was—and still is—the string quartet, made up of two violins (a first and a second), a viola, and a cello. The string quartet was especially popular with composers, because they could almost always find four string players to play their pieces. Franz Josef Haydn,

String quartet players listen to and watch each other to coordinate their playing without a conductor. Clockwise from front left are first violin, second violin, viola, and cello. A more usual arrangement has the cello and viola reversed.

an eighteenth-century Austrian composer, liked the string quartet so much that he wrote more than eighty pieces for it. There are other chamber-music groups that use stringed instruments; one almost as popular as the string quartet is the string trio, consisting of two violins and a cello, a violin, viola, and cello, or a violin, a cello, and a piano.

If you would like to hear what the instruments of the string section sound like—and be treated to some beautiful music at the same time—you might listen to records of these pieces:

FOR STRING ORCHESTRA
  Serenade in C, by the nineteenth-century Russian composer Peter Ilich Tchaikovsky
  Adagio for Strings, by the twentieth-century American composer Samuel Barber
FOR STRING QUARTET
  The Emperor Quartet, C major, Opus 74, No. 3, by the eighteenth-century Austrian composer Franz Josef Haydn
  Quartet No. 5, by the twentieth-century Hungarian composer Béla Bartók
FOR STRING TRIO
  String Trio No. 2, G major, Opus 9, No. 1, by the early nineteenth-century German composer Ludwig van Beethoven
FOR HARP
  Introduction and Allegro for harp, string quartet, flute, and clarinet, by the early twentieth-century French composer Maurice Ravel

THE WOODWIND SECTION

Sitting directly behind the string section is the woodwind section, so called because all the instruments use the player's breath, or wind, to produce their sound, and because at one time all of them were made of wood.

The woodwind section is much smaller than the string section. In most orchestras it includes only sixteen or seventeen players. Despite its size, however, the section is made up of many different kinds of instruments. Some of the woodwinds use a specially shaped mouthpiece to make the player's breath vibrate. Others have attached to the mouthpiece a little piece of cane or reed that vibrates when the player blows through the instrument. Still others have a mouthpiece formed of two little reeds tied around a steel tube.

All of the woodwinds produce notes of different pitch by lengthening or shortening the column of vibrating air trapped within the instrument. This is done by means of a set of keys that open or close little holes on the body of the instrument. To produce a high-pitched sound, the player opens almost all the holes, allowing air to escape and thereby shortening the column inside. To play a low note, he covers all the holes, and lengthens the air column.

There is something about the tone of any woodwind instrument—as with any string, brass, or percussion instrument—that identifies it as peculiarly "woodwind." We may not always be able to tell exactly what instrument we are hearing, but we can usually name its family. Yet each woodwind instrument—the flute, the piccolo, the clarinet, the oboe, the English horn, the saxophone, and the bassoon —has its own musical voice, and the woodwind section can produce many different musical sounds, or colors.

THE FLUTE

The flute is probably the oldest of all the woodwind instruments. The earliest flutes we know of were made by cavemen, thousands of years ago. The Greeks and the Romans, in their time, used flute music to provide a background for songs and poetry. Most of these early flutes were held upright and blown through one end like a whistle. Whistle-flutes also differed from the flute we use today in that they had no keys—just a set of eight little holes, which the player had to cover with the tips of his fingers. During the 1600's whistle-flutes called recorders were a part of the orchestra.

Both the flute and the piccolo (drawn to scale at left) require tricky finger-and-breath coordination from the player.

The modern, or transverse, flute is held horizontally instead of up and down, and the player blows across a hole in the side of the instrument instead of through the end. Except for the saxophone, which has a peculiar history of its own, the flute (along with its tiny counterpart, the piccolo) is the only woodwind instrument which is not still made of wood. Most flutes today are made of silver or nickel, but some have been made of gold and even platinum to produce a still brighter, purer tone.

The sound of the flute is clear and sweet. The lower notes are soft and mysterious, and the highest notes are louder and shrill. There are usually three flute players in an orchestra; the third flutist also plays the piccolo, switching from one instrument to the other when the music calls for it.

THE PICCOLO

The piccolo is the smallest instrument in the orchestra; it even takes its name from the Italian word meaning small. The piccolo is almost exactly like the flute, but only half as large. It is about a foot long and weighs only five or six ounces. Most piccolos today are made of silver, just like most flutes, but some piccolo players still use older instruments made of wood.

The range of the piccolo is much higher than that of the flute, and is in fact the highest range of any instrument. The tone of this little woodwind is shrill and piercing, and the piccolo is used often with the orchestra to add sparkle to the sound. Because of its size and peculiar musical voice, the piccolo has been humorously nicknamed the "imp of the orchestra."

THE OBOE

Although crude oboes have existed since ancient times in many lands, the oboe we know comes to us from India. During the Middle Ages travelers returning to Europe from the Orient brought with them some strange musical instruments. These little reed pipes, which the English named shawms, were used by the native Indian snake charmers to play their mysterious melodies. Their curious melancholy tone made them very popular in Europe, and soon instrument makers were turning out copies and improving on them until eventually the oboe was invented.

The modern oboe is about two feet long, and is made from cocuswood, a hard black wood found in South America. The mouthpiece is made from two pieces of cane, tied tightly around a small steel tube and then cut carefully to shape on one end. To produce a tone, the player places this shaped end between his lips and blows gently through the tiny opening between the pieces of cane. This kind of mouthpiece is called a double reed.

The oboe is a very difficult instrument to play. It has a delicate, complicated set of keys. It is also the hardest instrument in the orchestra to tune. For this reason most orchestras allow the oboe to supply their tuning note: when the oboist sounds his "A," the other players tune their instruments to match it. But the real problem of oboe playing lies in the tiny mouthpiece. The reeds are so narrow that it takes almost no air at all to make them vibrate, and the player has to take frequent breaths to renew the stale air in his lungs.

Though it is hard to play, the oboe is one of the most beautiful of all instruments to listen to. Its sound is soft,

A group of woodwinds from around 1650 includes (clockwise from front left) a shawm (early oboe), a fagotto (early bassoon), a zampogna (Italian bagpipe), a recorder (whistle-flute). The comical instrument on the floor is a serpent, despite its wooden body actually a forerunner of the tuba, the bass of the brass.

nasal, and a bit mournful. The oboe tone is so lovely that composers often include important solo parts for oboe in their orchestral works.

There are usually three oboists in an orchestra; the third oboist plays both the oboe and the English horn.

THE ENGLISH HORN

The strange thing about the English horn is that it is neither English nor a horn. It is just a big deep-voiced oboe, about one and a half times the size of the regular oboe and pitched five notes lower. The English horn developed from the Italian *oboe di caccia*, a large, loud oboe used in hunting and horseback riding. To make it easier to play on horseback, the body of this instrument was bent round into a series of curves or angles. In French, the instrument was called *cor anglé*, or angled horn, but the name was soon misspelled as *cor anglais*—English horn— and it has been the English horn ever since.

Like the oboe, the English horn is made of cocuswood and has a double-reed mouthpiece. Instead of being built in a series of curves, the modern horn has a curved mouthpiece. The bell, or bottom end, is bulb-shaped.

The English horn has a soft, smooth sound, somewhat deeper and fuller than that of the oboe. It is often given important melodic parts in orchestral compositions.

THE CLARINET

The clarinet is one of the most important members of the woodwind family; it has the widest range of any of the instruments. From a distance it looks very much like an oboe, but the clarinet has only one reed—a flat piece of cane, longer and wider than the oboe reed, attached to the mouthpiece by means of a little clamp.

Its single-reed mouthpiece makes the clarinet tone very different from that of the oboe. The lowest notes are rich and full, while the upper notes have a hard, bright sound. Most orchestras have at least three clarinetists, and sometimes extra players are used to double on bass clarinet and piccolo clarinet.

Our modern clarinet developed from a little French instrument called the chalumeau. During the Middle Ages, French peasants and shepherds used the chalumeau in their folk music, but it was not until 1780 that it had been improved enough to take its place in the orchestra. Therefore, much early orchestral music does not include parts for clarinet. In the twentieth century, however, the smooth tone and versatility of the clarinet have made it a popular instrument in dance bands and jazz groups.

THE BASS CLARINET

The bass clarinet is a large, deep-voiced clarinet, twice the size of the regular clarinet and pitched eight notes lower. Most bass clarinets are made of wood, and have a large, curved metal bell.

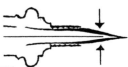

The three basic reed mouthpieces of woodwind instruments are, from top to bottom opposite, the oboe double-reed mouthpiece, the clarinet single-reed, and the bassoon double-reed. The diagrams at right show the oboe reeds in closed position and in open position with air being directed between them.

The oboe, the English horn, and the clarinet, despite their similar appearance, differ in range, versatility, and tone quality.

The bass clarinet is used only occasionally with the orchestra. Its tone adds fullness and depth to the sound of the woodwind section.

THE PICCOLO CLARINET

The name of this instrument tells us exactly what it is— the piccolo of the clarinet family, small and high-pitched. The piccolo clarinet looks like its larger clarinet relatives, but it is only two thirds the size of the regular clarinet and is pitched four notes higher. Its sharp, squeaky tone adds a bright sound to the woodwind section.

THE SAXOPHONE

The newest instrument to join the woodwind section is the saxophone, invented in 1839 by a Belgian instrument maker named Adolphe Sax. Sax started with an instrument called an ophicleide—a kind of tuba with keys—and attached a clarinet mouthpiece to it. The result was a very strange instrument indeed. Its body was made of brass instead of wood. It had a clarinet mouthpiece and reed, but the system of keys was different from that of the clarinet.

The unique thing about this new instrument was its sound. The low notes were mellow and breathy, while the high notes were bright and sweet-sounding. Sax built his invention in seven different sizes to form a whole family of instruments. The largest of these, the contrabass saxophone, is about six and a half feet tall. The smallest, the sopranino, is only sixteen inches long. Most saxophones are built with a curved bell and mouthpipe (the metal tube connecting the mouthpiece to the body of the instrument), like bass clarinets, but sometimes the two smallest sizes are built straight, like regular clarinets.

The French composer Georges Bizet was fascinated by the saxophone after seeing one at the Paris International Exhibition in 1867, and included it as a curiosity in a new composition. This early use was not followed up, however. It was not until the early twentieth century that the saxophone was really admitted to the orchestra, and it is still not a fully accepted member. Instead, the various saxophones have become important in jazz and popular-music groups. The sax is probably best known for its use in blues music, for which the jazz saxophonist draws loud plaintive wails from his instrument.

THE BASSOON

In Italian, the word for bassoon is *fagotto,* which means "bundle of sticks." This is just what the bassoon looks like—two big sticks tied together side by side. It is actually a single tube of hard maple wood, eight feet long but doubled over once to make it easier to hold.

The bassoon is really a bass oboe, four times as long as the regular oboe. Like the oboe, it uses a double reed. The reed is attached to the top of the instrument by a long silver tube called a bocal. The modern bassoon has more keys on it than any wind instrument—twenty-two in all.

The alto saxophone is one of the middle-sized instruments of the saxophone family. Its smaller, higher-pitched brothers are the soprano and the sopranino; ranged below it are the tenor, baritone, bass, and contrabass.

The sound of the bassoon is quite comical, and has earned the instrument the nickname "clown of the orchestra." The lowest notes have a rough, awkward sound, while the higher register has a funny buzzing quality. The bassoon, with the deep full tone of its middle range, strengthens the over-all sound of the woodwind section. There are usually three bassoonists in the orchestra, with the third bassoonist also doubling on the contrabassoon.

THE CONTRABASSOON

The contrabassoon, or double bassoon, is the largest instrument in the woodwind section. It resembles the bassoon, but is twice as long and pitched eight notes lower. Because it is so large, and much too heavy to be held by the player, the contrabassoon has a metal spike on the bottom for resting the instrument on the floor.

The contrabassoon has the lowest range of any instrument in the orchestra. Its tone is very much like that of the bassoon, but much lower and more raspy. In the orchestra, the contrabassoon adds a deep, strong bottom to the sound of the woodwind section.

Each of the woodwinds requires a particular skill from the player. The deep-voiced bassoon, more than the others, takes a lot of breath.

WOODWIND GROUPS

When woodwinds play apart from the orchestra they almost always play in combination with other types of instruments. Some string chamber groups include one or more woodwind instruments, and woodwinds with brass is a frequent combination, as we shall see later on after our introduction to the brass section. Even what we call a *woodwind* group, though it is made up primarily of woodwinds, normally contains one outsider: the French horn. The woodwind quintet, for instance, has five instruments —a flute, a clarinet, an oboe, a bassoon, and a French horn. The French horn, of course is a *brass* wind, but its sound blends so well with the other instruments that it has always been a part of the group. During the 1700's, many little pieces called serenades were composed for the woodwind quintet.

Listening to records of the following compositions is an enjoyable way of getting to know the instruments of the woodwind family:

FOR WOODWINDS WITH BRASS SUPPORT
  Serenade for Thirteen Wind Instruments, by the late nineteenth–early twentieth-century Austrian composer Richard Strauss
FOR WOODWIND QUINTET
  Kleine Kammermusik, Opus 24, No. 2, by the twentieth-century German composer Paul Hindemith
FOR WOODWIND QUARTET AND STRING ORCHESTRA
  Sinfonia Concertante, E flat major, K. App. 9 (297b), by the eighteenth-century Austrian composer Wolfgang Amadeus Mozart

THE BRASS WIND SECTION

The brass wind section of the orchestra takes its name from the fact that all its instruments are made of metal, usually brass, and that they all use the player's breath to produce musical sound. The basic method may be the same as for woodwinds, but it generally takes a good deal more lung power to play a brass instrument—as anyone who has tried to get just one clear tone out of a trumpet knows.

Instead of a reed or a flute mouthpiece like the woodwinds, the brass instruments have a cup-shaped mouthpiece. The lips of the player take the place of the reed; the player makes them vibrate against the mouthpiece.

Early brass instruments could play only a few notes. To overcome these limits, the players used pieces of tubing of different lengths to vary the length of the air column within their instrument, thereby changing the tuning and enabling them to get more notes. These tubes, called crooks, were fitted between the mouthpiece and body of the instrument. To change the tuning, the player had to stop playing, change crooks as quickly as possible, and then find his place in the music. Early brass players must have looked very much like plumbers as they carried their instruments and a bag of seven or eight crooks to a concert.

In the early 1800's a German bandmaster named Heinrich Stoelzel invented a new kind of brass instrument, which had three crooks already attached to it. The player

Town bands like this one from the early 1500's used to play for celebrations and official events. The instruments, a mixture of brass, woodwind, and percussion, are a drum, two fifes (early transverse flutes), a trumpet, three sackbuts (early trombones), and a shawm.

could use any of the crooks, or all of them, just by pushing a set of little keys called valves. Stoelzel's invention was a great boon to brass players, who could now change crooks without missing any notes. Soon almost all the instruments of the brass section were being constructed this way.

THE FRENCH HORN

The most important instrument of the brass section is the French horn. Its history goes back to the Middle Ages, when round horns without valves were used in France and Italy for hunting calls. These early horns had such a clear, pretty sound that they soon became popular members of the orchestra.

The modern French horn is a narrow tube of brass or silver, sixteen feet long, ending in a large, flaring bell and

The very long column of vibrating air in the French horn gives the instrument its full, strong tone.

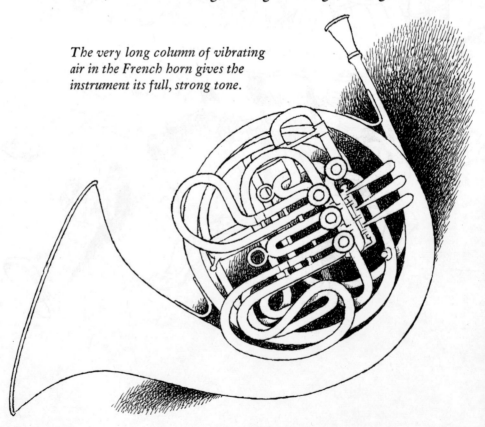

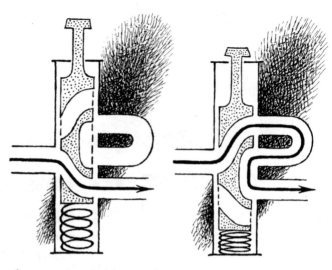

These trumpet valves demonstrate how all brass valves operate. The raised valve lets air pass directly through. Lowering the valve detours the air through the little crook, or valve slide, lengthening the total air column and changing the pitch.

coiled round and round to form a circular horn about two feet across. Like most of the brass instruments, the French horn has three valves.

The French horn has a wonderful variety of tone colors. The horn player can change the sound himself just by moving his hand around inside the bell. The low notes of the horn are muffled and mysterious-sounding, the middle range is clear and powerful, while the highest notes are very bright.

The beautiful tone of the French horn has made it a favorite instrument of composers. The clarity of its middle and upper ranges blends well with both the woodwind and brass instruments. Orchestral music is usually written with four different horn parts, and most orchestras use at least six or eight French horns.

THE TRUMPET

The trumpet is probably the oldest member of the brass family. The trumpets mentioned in the Bible and the trumpets used by the Roman armies, except for the addition of valves, were not very different from the trumpet that is used in the orchestra today.

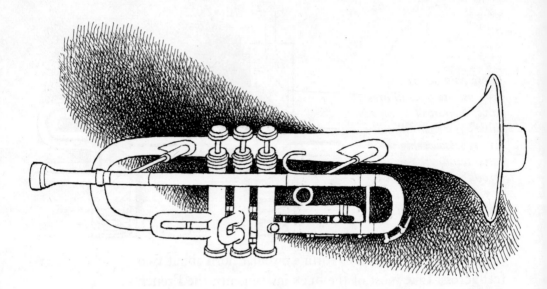

The agile, bright-sounding trumpet is probably the best-known of the brass instruments. Here it is shown with its mute in place inside the bell.

The modern trumpet is a tube of brass or silver about eight feet long, with a small bell. To make it easier to carry, this tube is bent round several times to form an elongated coil. Like the other members of the brass family, the trumpet has three valves.

The usual trumpet sound is brassy and brilliant, and quite loud; it is a natural choice for marches and military music. For certain musical passages the trumpet player may place a mute in the bell of his instrument, making the tone very soft and thin. It is not easy to produce a strong, steady note on the trumpet. Good lungs and jaw muscles are needed to tame this stubborn instrument.

There are usually three trumpeters in a symphony orchestra. Two other instruments very much like the trumpet are the cornet and the fluegelhorn. They are commonly used in bands but seldom included in the orchestra.

THE CORNET

The Italian word *cornetto,* from which the cornet takes its name, means little horn. From a distance, the cornet looks very much like a trumpet; it too is made of brass or silver and has three valves. But the tube of the cornet is shorter and wider than that of the trumpet. This difference makes the cornet much easier to blow and results in a softer, mellower tone.

The cornet is popular as a band instrument. When used with the orchestra, it is played by the regular trumpeters.

THE FLUEGELHORN

The fluegelhorn is a large, heavy trumpet. Like the other members of the trumpet family, it is made of brass or silver and has three valves. But the fluegelhorn is much larger and wider than either the trumpet or the cornet, and its sound is loud and blaring.

The fluegelhorn is really a band instrument and only rarely finds a place in the orchestra.

THE EUPHONIUM

The euphonium is a large, coiled brass instrument, pitched eight notes below the trumpet. Most euphoniums have three valves, but some have a special fourth valve to lower the range still further. The sound of the instrument is rich and smooth.

Euphoniums are regular members of bands. In the orchestra they sometimes pinch-hit on high parts for the tuba, a deep-voiced brass with a very troublesome upper range.

THE TROMBONE

The trombone, or slide trombone, takes its name from the Italian *trombone*, which means large trumpet. It is a long narrow brass tube, twice as long as the trumpet, bent round and ending in a small bell. But there is one way in which the trombone differs from all the other members of the brass section. It has no valves at all. Instead, it has a long slide—an extra tube fitted into the main one—which the player moves back and forth to change the pitch of the instrument.

The trombone, like the euphonium, is pitched eight notes below the trumpet. Its sound is deep and powerful, but not as mellow as that of the euphonium. It helps to give body to the sound of the brass section. There are usually three trombonists in an orchestra. The third trombonist often plays the bass trombone, a very large trombone with a little valve that lowers the range four notes.

The trombone is a very old instrument, and has changed little since the Middle Ages. A great deal of music has been

Playing the trombone is a feat of lung power—and arm length. The instrument is shown here with its slide all the way in. Full extension would bring it out nearly twice as far.

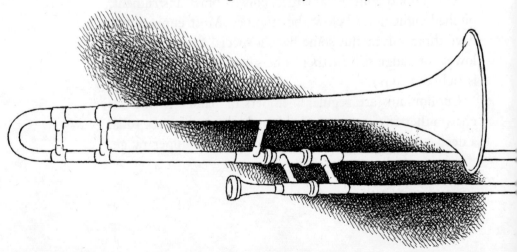

written for it; almost all the orchestral music of the last two hundred years includes parts for this popular instrument.

THE TUBA

Just carrying around his instrument is a hard chore for the tuba player. The heavy, cumbersome tuba is the largest of all the brass. If its tube were unrolled and laid out straight, it would measure about thirty-five feet end to end. The tuba is also the lowest-voiced of the brass; it is pitched eight notes below the trombone and the euphonium. Most tubas have three valves, but some have four and even five valves to extend their range still lower.

The sound of the tuba is deep, rumbling, and gruff, adding a full rich bottom to the sound of the brass section. There is usually only one tuba player in the orchestra.

THE BAND AND OTHER WIND GROUPS

The brass and woodwind instruments often play apart from the orchestra in various combinations. The largest of these groups is the band, which is made up of all the members of the woodwind and brass sections. A band may have only twenty-five players, or well over a hundred. Many high schools and now even grade schools have their own bands, which give concerts, march in parades, and play at football games. There is nothing that sparks the excitement of a festive occasion like a good rousing number from the band.

Another popular group is the brass choir, composed of only brass instruments and a few drums. Composers have

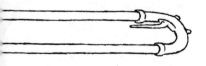

been writing for the brass choir since the Middle Ages.

The brass quartet is the smallest of all the brass wind groups. Most brass quartets contain two trumpets and two trombones, but some substitute a French horn for one of the trombones.

Brass instruments, of course, play in partnership with string, woodwind, and percussion instruments as well. The French horn in particular really gets around—we have already seen how it has found its way into the woodwind quintet.

The following pieces make a fine introduction to the sound of brass instruments and wind groups:

Drums, piccolos, trumpets, French horns, trombones, and tubas make up this modern marching band. At back is a sousaphone, a tuba made for marching, named after composer John Philip Sousa.

FOR BAND
"The Stars and Stripes Forever," by the late nineteenth–early twentieth-century American composer John Philip Sousa

First Suite for Military Band, by the late nineteenth–early twentieth-century English composer Gustav Holst

FOR BRASS CHOIR
Fanfare for the Common Man, by the twentieth-century American composer Aaron Copland

FOR BRASS QUARTET
Canzona per Sonar a Quattro, No. 4, by the sixteenth-century Italian composer Giovanni Gabrieli

WIND INSTRUMENTS WITH THE FULL ORCHESTRA
"Till Eulenspiegel's Merry Pranks," by the late nineteenth–early twentieth-century Austrian composer Richard Strauss

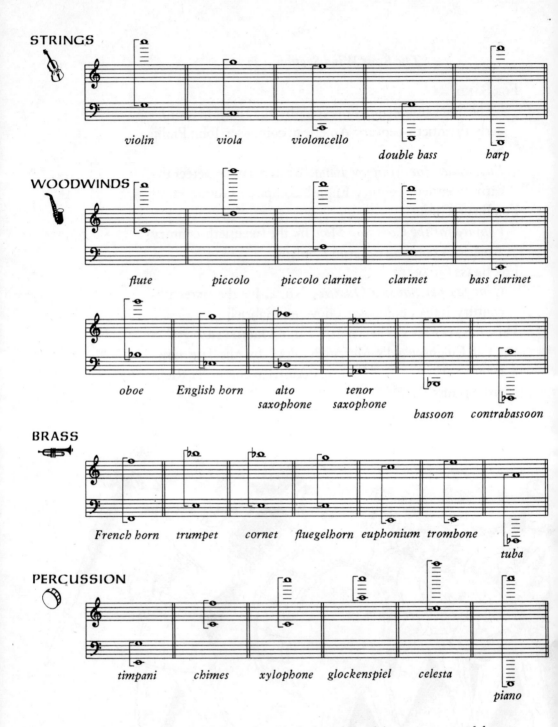

The ranges of the major pitched orchestral instruments—and how they compare—are shown here. The written notes represent the highest and lowest tones each instrument is capable of playing; an instrument's range includes all the notes in between.

THE PERCUSSION SECTION

Seated or standing toward the rear of the stage, behind the strings and winds, are the percussion players. The instruments of this section all produce sound when their parts are struck together or hit with special hammers. Of all the orchestral instruments, the percussion are the oldest. Even before men knew how to make music by blowing through a reed, or plucking a bow string, they made a kind of music by hitting two sticks together or banging on a hollow log.

There are many different kinds of percussion instruments, but only a certain few normally find a place in the orchestra. These are the timpani, the chimes, the xylophone, the glockenspiel, the celesta, the piano, the snare drum, the bass drum, the cymbals, the triangle, and the gong.

THE TIMPANI

The timpani are the only drums that can be tuned to a musical pitch. The other drums in the orchestra produce uneven vibrations, so their sounds are not really musical tones.

The timpani come to us from the Middle Ages, when Crusaders returning from the Holy Land brought with them large kettle-shaped drums. These early drums were usually used in pairs, tied across the backs of horses. Our

Arab armies of the Middle Ages used kettledrums to signal their troops. The drums were tuned by adjusting the ropes extending from the head. The orchestral timpanist at right, using special handles, tunes each drum to a different pitch. He may have to retune in the middle of a piece when other notes are needed.

timpani today are similar to those ancient drums, as their alternate name, kettledrums, indicates. They are quite large, and look like big copper kettles.

Across the top of each drum is a tightly stretched piece of calfskin called the head. To play the timpani, the drummer strikes the head with a pair of little sticks called mallets. Some mallets have round pieces of felt on the end, others are wrapped with yarn, and some are solid wood. Each kind of mallet makes a different sound, and a player often has to use several different sets in the course of the same piece of music.

To tune the timpani, the player adjusts the tension on the calfskin head, easing or increasing it in order to lower or raise the pitch. Some timpani have a set of handles which tighten the head by pushing a big steel ring down on it. Others have a large foot pedal which moves the ring by means of a whole system of rods and levers. Unlike string or wind instruments, the timpani will play only the one basic note to which they are tuned. There is no way for the timpanist to change pitch without retuning.

The timpani sound is deep and resonant. While there is usually only one timpanist with the orchestra, he may use a set of two, three, four, or even five drums. The timpani are probably the most important members of the percussion section. They are used more often with the orchestra than any other percussion instrument.

THE CHIMES

In appearance, as well as in sound, the chimes are an unusual instrument. They consist of a set of thirteen long tubes of brass or nickel-silver, which hang on thick leather loops from a large metal rack. The player strikes the tubes with a small hard leather mallet, producing a deep, clear, resounding tone. In the orchestra, the chimes are often used to imitate church bells.

THE XYLOPHONE

The xylophone has a unique sound, very hard and bright. It is used very often in modern music, and especially for popular music and jazz.

The instrument consists of a set of small wooden bars on a flat rack that the player strikes with a set of mallets. Xylophone mallets are different from timpani mallets; they are long and thin, with little round heads of yarn or hard rubber. The xylophone player may use four mallets at the same time, holding two in each hand.

THE GLOCKENSPIEL

The glockenspiel looks like a small xylophone. But instead of wooden bars, the glockenspiel has bars of metal, usually nickel or silver. The instrument is played with a set of hard rubber mallets like those of the xylophone. Its high, tinkling tone brightens the orchestral sound.

The percussion section includes some bulky machinery. From back to front are chimes, xylophone, celesta, and glockenspiel.

THE CELESTA

The celesta looks like a tiny piano. It has a small key-board with, usually, thirty-six black and white keys. These keys strike a set of tuned metal plates inside a kind of echo chamber which prolongs the sound of each note. The soft, sweet tone of the celesta has attracted many composers to include parts for it in their orchestral music.

THE PIANO

The piano is the largest percussion instrument and, indeed, the king of all the instruments. The organ may surpass it in size, but not in versatility and popularity. Although the piano sound is produced by vibrating strings, the method by which they are made to vibrate classes the instrument as a member of the percussion family. Small felt-covered hammers connected to the keyboard strike against the strings when the pianist depresses the keys.

Our modern piano developed from an instrument called the psaltery, which is so ancient that it is even mentioned in the Old Testament. The psaltery was a metal frame, shaped like a triangle, with a set of thin metal strings stretched tightly across it. Each string was tuned to a different pitch, and the instrument was played by striking the strings with mallets or plucking them with hooks.

During the Middle Ages someone placed the psaltery in a box to serve as a sounding chamber, and added a small keyboard. The keys of the keyboard were connected to levers, which released little metal hammers called tangents to fly up and strike the strings from below. This new instrument was called the clavichord. The clavichord became enormously popular and fashionable in sixteenth-century society, but it had one shortcoming: in a big room you could hardly hear it.

Soon a new instrument, called the harpsichord, was invented. It looked like a large clavichord, but in place of hammers it had little pieces of leather or goose quill that flew up and plucked the strings. This made a much louder and fuller sound but one that faded away very quickly.

Around 1700 another new instrument came on the scene.

Invented by an Italian harpsichord maker named Barto-
lomeo Cristofori, it combined the best advantages of its two
forerunners. It did away with the plucking mechanism of
the harpsichord and substituted felt-covered hammers
which struck the strings to produce a full, lasting tone.
The new instrument also had a set of pedals that helped
the artist at the keyboard control the loudness or softness
of his playing. The inventors therefore named their instrument *pianoforte*, from the Italian words for soft and
loud. As time went by, musicians began to call it simply
the piano, and with some few additional improvements it
is the same instrument that we know today.

The piano is not usually considered a part of the orchestra. It is played either as a solo instrument, as part of a
chamber group, or in pieces called piano concertos as the
featured instrument in a kind of partnership with the whole
orchestra.

*Tone is produced in the modern piano by means of the "double
action" mechanism. Pressing the key sets in motion the trigger
mechanism, throwing the felt-covered hammer up to strike the
string. Simultaneously, the key end raises the damper, allowing
the string to vibrate freely. When the key is released, the damper
falls back, stopping the string vibrations.*

The piano's first ancestor, the psaltery (a), had no keyboard at all. The clavichord (c), a keyboard instrument with no legs, was placed on a table or on the player's lap. Harpsichords came in three different sizes—the triangular tabletop virginal (b), the wing-shaped spinet (e), and the true harpsichord (d), which had the modern grand piano shape and often two keyboards with two sets of strings. The early piano (f) had a smaller keyboard than today's large grand (g) with its eighty-eight keys and three pedals.

THE SNARE DRUM

The snare drum is the smallest drum used with the orchestra. It is only about sixteen inches across. Instead of one head, like the timpani, the snare drum has two heads of calfskin or plastic stretched tightly over each end of its shell. The bottom head has several steel wires called snares running across it. When the upper head is struck with a pair of hard wood drumsticks these snares bounce against the lower head and make a rattling sound.

Jazz groups use orchestral instruments and some of their own as well. Along with the percussion, tenor sax, trumpet, and bass in this group is an electric guitar.

With the orchestra, the snare drum is used in loud passages to strengthen the sound of the percussion section. The head of the instrument is taut and springy and therefore very responsive to rapid hammering by an agile drummer. Composers often write fast, difficult parts for the snare drum.

THE BASS DRUM

The bass drum is a very large drum with two calfskin heads like the snare drum, but no snares. The bass drum used with the orchestra is usually four or five feet across, and because of its size must be played standing up on its edge. Instead of using a mallet or a wood drumstick, the player uses a special beater that has a soft woolen tip. The sound of the bass drum is very deep and booming.

THE CYMBALS

The cymbals are two large brass plates, each about two feet across. The player holds each cymbal by means of a leather loop tied through a tiny hole in the center. To play the cymbals, the player strikes them together with a quick up-and-down movement. This makes a loud metallic crash. Then, to stop them from ringing, he presses them against his body. Sometimes only one cymbal is used. It is hung from a rack by its loop, and struck with a mallet to make an eerie, brassy sound like a gong.

A composition with a lot of passages for percussion will keep these two busy. The man in front is responsible for the bass drum, snare drum, and triangle; the man at back for the cymbals and gong.

Cymbals of various kinds go back many hundreds of years. The kind in use today comes to us from Turkey, and did not become part of the orchestra until about 1780, when Turkish music became popular in Europe. Even today, the best cymbals are made in Turkey.

THE TRIANGLE

The triangle is probably the simplest instrument in the whole orchestra. It is a small metal bar, bent into the shape which gives it its name. It is hung from a music stand by a little loop of silk thread. When the player strikes the triangle with a little metal rod it makes a high, clear note like a tiny bell.

The triangle is used sparingly in the orchestra, for special effects or to brighten the full orchestra sound.

THE GONG

The gong comes to us from China. It is a large brass plate, four or five feet across and so heavy it must be hung from a rack by a thick leather strap. It is played with a wool-tipped beater like that used for the bass drum. When struck softly, the sound of the gong is deep and mysterious. When it is struck with more force it makes a loud, resounding peal.

PERCUSSION PLAYING

It might seem from our discussion of percussion instruments that the percussion players of the orchestra have a very easy time of it. After all, they need only bang on their instruments to make music. But this is not really so. The right kind of bang, at the right time, takes skill. Most orchestras have only three percussionists, and one of these plays only the timpani. This leaves two players to play all the other instruments in the section. A good percussionist must know how to play them all.

The next time you go to an orchestra concert, be sure to watch the players in the percussion section. Their instruments are lined up in a long row around the back of the orchestra. If the music requires many instruments at the same time, there may be several extra players.

Many modern composers have written music for percussion instruments alone. A recital of percussion music is always interesting to listen to, and it is a good chance to see percussionists at work.

The pieces listed below offer an exciting introduction to the sound of the percussion instruments:

Music for Strings, Percussion, and Celesta, by the twentieth-century Hungarian composer Béla Bartók
Concerto for Percussion and Small Orchestra, by the twentieth-century French composer Darius Milhaud
Ionization, by the twentieth-century French composer Edgar Varèse
Concerto for Pianoforte and Orchestra, C major, K. 503, by the eighteenth-century Austrian composer Wolfgang Amadeus Mozart

Paintings of Egyptian orchestras have been found on the walls of ancient tombs. This group from about 1000 B.C. includes two harps, a flute, and an instrument like a guitar. Musicians at this time were usually slaves.

THE ORCHESTRA
THROUGH THE AGES

It is very hard to say just how and when the great symphony orchestra we know today came to be. As long as men have made music, they have enjoyed playing together. We can imagine a group of cavemen, many thousands of years ago, tootling on simple whistles and beating primitive drums. This was really the first orchestra. The drum and flute orchestras of many primitive tribes today give us a good idea of what this early music must have been like.

Gradually music-making became more complex. We have paintings from the time of the ancient Egyptians, showing orchestras of harps, flutes, and percussion instruments that were used to accompany dancing. We know that the ancient Romans and Greeks had orchestral background music for plays and religious ceremonies.

During the Middle Ages, the most important music was the music of the Church. The pipe organ was just being developed and was not yet a very reliable instrument, so many early composers wrote music for groups of instruments to help out the organ. Because every church did not have the same number of musicians, or the same selection of instruments, composers could not assign a particular instrument to each of the parts. One of these early orchestras might have been made up of four viols, two recorders, an oboe, a trumpet, two trombones, and of course, the pipe organ; it all depended on what was available.

The organist in this early eighteenth-century church orchestra is conducting from the keyboard. The large stringed instrument nearest him is a bass lute; the other strings are all viols. The curved woodwind at left is a krummhorn.

Many kings and noblemen also had small groups of musicians to play for their enjoyment at court. Like the church orchestras, these early court orchestras were made up of any musicians who happened to be in residence or working at the court at the time. Therefore, a court orchestra might have as many as nineteen or twenty players or as few as five or six, and any combination of instruments was possible. At this time, in fact, there was no clear distinction between an orchestra and a chamber group.

By the early 1600's, orchestras were growing larger and better, and their development had become quite separate from the development of chamber groups. Composers were beginning to write for particular combinations of instruments, like the string quartet. When they wrote for a larger group—for the orchestra—they also specified the kind and number of instruments for each written part.

In the orchestra of the 1600's, the most important instrument was the harpsichord. In fact, the whole orchestra was built around the harpsichord and the low stringed instruments because they supplied a solid foundation for the rest of the orchestra. The harpsichord parts were written in a kind of musical shorthand called figured bass, and the harpsichordist was responsible for filling them out.

As time went by, the harpsichord became less popular and lost its central role in the orchestra. In 1745 a group of German composers was asked to form an orchestra for the court of a German nobleman. The result, consisting of thirty-nine instruments, including eighteen violins, six violas, four cellos, two double basses, two flutes, two oboes, two French horns, two trumpets, and timpani, was really the first modern orchestra.

It was at this time that the word symphony—which had

long been used casually for all types of compositions—began to mean a particular kind of long orchestral piece in several movements. The symphony became the most characteristic composition for orchestra, and we still think of it as such. This probably accounts for our term "symphony orchestra," which simply means the orchestra as it is usually organized for an orchestral concert, rather than for an opera or ballet performance.

During the 1900's more and more instruments were added to the orchestra, until finally an Austrian composer, Richard Strauss, wrote a piece called *Alpine Symphony* for a huge orchestra of 130 players. After that, people began to see the folly of letting the orchestra grow to such proportions. Most of our orchestras today are made up of about eighty-five musicians.

As the composition of the orchestra changed, its sound changed. You can follow the development of the orchestra through its various stages by listening to these records:

THE EARLY COURT (RENAISSANCE) ORCHESTRA
Overture to *Orfeo,* by the Italian composer Claudio Monteverdi (1567-1643)
Sacrae Symphoniae, by the Italian composer Giovanni Gabrieli (1557-1612)
THE HARPSICHORD (BAROQUE) ORCHESTRA
Brandenburg Concerto, No. 3, G major, by the German composer Johann Sebastian Bach (1685-1750)
THE EARLY SYMPHONY (CLASSICAL) ORCHESTRA
Symphony No. 45, F sharp minor, by the Austrian composer Franz Josef Haydn (1732-1809)
Symphony No. 1, C major, by the German composer Ludwig van Beethoven (1770-1827)

THE NINETEENTH-CENTURY (ROMANTIC) ORCHESTRA
  "Siegfried's Rhine Journey," by the German composer Richard Wagner (1813-1883)
  Symphony No. 4, F minor, by the German composer Johannes Brahms (1833-1897)

THE MODERN (TWENTIETH-CENTURY) ORCHESTRA
  The Fire Bird Suite, by the Russian composer Igor Stravinsky (1882-   )
  Symphony No. 5, by the Russian composer Dimitri Shostakovich (1906-   )

A wonderful piece by a living English composer, based on a tune by another English composer, Henry Purcell, who wrote three centuries earlier, is Benjamin Britten's *Young Person's Guide to the Orchestra*. Every orchestral instrument, in turn, is given a good long say before they all play together. It's a fine way to learn to identify the individual voices of the orchestra.

Each conductor arranges his orchestra as he thinks best. The seating plan shown here, however, is the one most generally used.

THE RISE OF THE CONDUCTOR

When the earliest musical groups were formed they were so small that it was very easy for the musicians to stay together in playing their music. But during the Middle Ages musicians found that they needed someone to coordinate them and lead them through the music. This was the origin of the conductor. Early conductors often waved a big roll of music in one hand to indicate the speed, or tempo, of the piece. Others beat the tempo on the floor with a heavy metal staff. This way of conducting could be very dangerous, and at least one early conductor crushed his foot in the process.

When the harpsichord was the most important instrument of the orchestra, the conductor often played the figured-bass part on the harpsichord and beat time with his right hand whenever he could. Later orchestras were conducted by the first violinist, who would start the music by directing for a moment with his bow, then play along with the group. As orchestras grew larger and larger, and music more difficult, the musicians found that they needed a conductor to lead them all the way through the piece, so the first violinist became concertmaster and a full-time conductor took his place. This happened toward the end of the eighteenth century.

From casual observation you might think the conductor has the easiest or at least the most enjoyable job in the or-

This page from the score of Georges Enesco's Rumanian Rhapsody No. 1 *(used by permission of Edward B. Marks Music Corp.) shows a conductor's notes to himself on interpretation.*

chestra. It is very hard to tell from merely his arm motions and occasional facial gestures just how difficult and important his job really is. But the conductor's job is very hard; in fact he must work harder than any member of the orchestra.

The conductor has to lead the orchestra through the music and keep everyone playing smoothly together. To do this, he must know each player's part as thoroughly as if he had to perform it himself. As an aid, the conductor has a kind of master copy of the music, called the score, with all the parts written out on separate lines. While the player is reading only one or two lines of music at a time, the conductor has to read as many as thirty-five lines at once.

This by itself is a very hard job, but it is not all that the conductor must do. All the members of the orchestra depend on the conductor to show them how fast or slow the music is going, and how loud to play. He does this by means of a complicated set of hand signals. In his right hand, he holds a stick called the baton. He moves the baton at a certain speed, to show the musicians the tempo. By raising or lowering his left hand, he shows them how loud to play. He must also help them to start and stop together and to enter on cue in the course of a piece.

But the most essential thing the conductor does is decide how the music will be played, what the music will say. This is called interpretation. When he interprets a score, the conductor does his best to re-create the music as he thinks the composer would like to hear it. He must decide what parts are most important, and balance the orchestra sound so that the audience can hear those parts even if they are being played very softly.

To do all these things well, the conductor and the orchestra have to practice together often. In rehearsals the conductor helps the musicians learn the hard parts of the music, and the musicians begin to know how the conductor wants the music played. So you can see that the conductor has the most crucial and challenging job in the orchestra, and can understand why it takes years and years of study and practice to become a good conductor.

And now let's get back to the concert, where the musicians are still warming up on stage. Violinists, bassoonists, trombone players, and timpanists—all create a bewildering jumble of sound. A cellist stops to tighten his bow, a clarinetist fusses with his reed, and a horn player folds back the corners of the pages in his score so that they can be quickly turned. Then for a moment everything is quiet. The oboist sounds his tuning note, and each musician plays a note or two to be sure he has his pitch adjusted correctly.

There is another moment of silence. The lights dim, and then we begin to applaud as we see the conductor walking out to his place in front of the orchestra, mounting the platform, and turning to face the players. He raises his baton. The violinists tuck their instruments under their chins, the wind players bring their mouthpieces to their lips. . . . And now, *music!*

GLOSSARY OF MUSICAL TERMS

bell: the flaring end section of a wind instrument

bow: the wooden stick strung with horsehair that is drawn across the strings of an instrument to produce sound. The way in which a bow is used—its direction and speed—is called bowing.

bridge: the thin piece of wood that supports the strings of instruments of the violin family

classical music: music of a serious (though not necessarily unhumorous) nature, such as symphonies, operas, concertos, sonatas, and tone poems. Classical music can also refer specifically to music of the eighteenth century, such as Mozart's.

clavichord: a keyboard instrument in which little metal wedges strike the strings to make sound

concertmaster: the head of the first violin section who acts as leader of the string section of the orchestra

figured bass: the musical shorthand used by early keyboard instrument players. The bass notes were written out, and above them were symbols and numbers to guide the player in filling in the upper parts.

hammers: the felt-covered pieces of wood that strike the strings of the piano

harmony: two or more tones sounded at the same time

harpsichord: a keyboard instrument in which the strings are plucked by quill or leather

intensity, or volume: the loudness or softness of sound

interval: the distance between two notes. Intervals are usually named by numbers, for instance a third (three notes), or a seventh (seven notes). An interval of eight notes is called an octave.

jazz: music that developed around 1900 from the music of the American Negro. Much of jazz music is not written down, but is made up, or improvised, by the player as he goes along.

keyboard: the row of keys on instruments of the piano and organ family. By pressing on them, the player operates the sound-making mechanism inside.

mallets: sticks with tips of felt or hard rubber used in playing percussion instruments

mouthpiece: the part of a wind instrument which is placed either in the player's mouth or against his lips so air can be directed through it

movement: a large section of a musical composition, which may last from three to fifteen minutes. Orchestral symphonies have three or four separate movements.

mute: a device that can be attached to an instrument to make the sound softer

note: a tone of a particular pitch. Also, the written symbol for a tone.

organ: the largest of the keyboard instruments. Instead of having strings like the other keyboard instruments, the organ has tubes of varying lengths in which air is made to vibrate to produce sound.

pedal: a foot-operated lever controlling different functions on different instruments. On the harp, for instance, pedals change the tuning of the strings; on the piano, pedals sustain or alter the quality of the piano tone.

pitch: the highness or lowness of a musical sound

"pops": concert music of a light nature, such as music from Broadway shows, operettas, and films

psaltery: an instrument from biblical times, consisting of a triangular frame with strings stretched across it and played with a pair of mallets or with hooks

range: the distance between the highest and lowest notes of a particular instrument; hence, all the notes an instrument is capable of playing

recorders: the family of whistle-flutes popular from the Middle Ages until about 1725, when they were replaced in the orchestra by the transverse flute. Recorders were made in six different sizes.

resonant: describing sound that is prolonged, rich, and ringing. A *resonant* instrument, such as the cello, is constructed so that it characteristically produces resonant tones.

score: the "master copy" of a musical composition which the conductor uses to follow the parts of all the individual instruments

solo: a featured or important part written for one instrument

symphony: a large, complex composition for orchestra, usually in four movements

tempo: the speed at which a piece of music is played

tone: a musical sound, that is a sound having the same number of vibrations each second

troubadours: traveling poets, singers, and musicians of the Middle Ages

tuning up: the adjustment of instruments so that their pitches are correct, or in tune

valves: mechanical devices that permit brass players to vary the tuning of their instruments

viols: a family of early bowed string instruments from which our modern violin family developed